MW01268571

GARAGE
BANDS™

HOW TO PRODUCE, RELEASE, AND MARKET YOUR MUSIC

HEATHER HASAN

rosen publishing's
rosen
central®

NEW YORK

To Samuel, Matthew, and Sarah—my own little rock band. For all the spontaneous jam sessions that have broken out in my living room.

Published in 2012 by The Rosen Publishing Group, Inc.
29 East 21st Street, New York, NY 10010

First Edition

Library of Congress Cataloging-in-Publication Data

Hasan, Heather.
How to produce, release, and market your music/Heather Hasan.—1st ed.
    p. cm.—(Garage bands)
Includes bibliographical references and index.
ISBN 978-1-4488-5658-9 (library binding)—
ISBN 978-1-4488-5662-6 (pbk.)—
ISBN 978-1-4488-5666-4 (6-pack)
1. Music—Vocational guidance—Juvenile literature.
2. Sound recordings—Production and direction—Juvenile literature.
3. Music trade—Juvenile literature.
4. Music—Marketing—Juvenile literature. I. Title.
ML3795.H34 2012
780.23—dc22

                                                        2011015278

Manufactured in the United States of America

CPSIA Compliance Information: Batch #W12YA: For further information, contact Rosen Publishing, New York, New York, at 1-800-237-9932.

On the cover: A musician uses sound mixing equipment to produce music.

CONTENTS

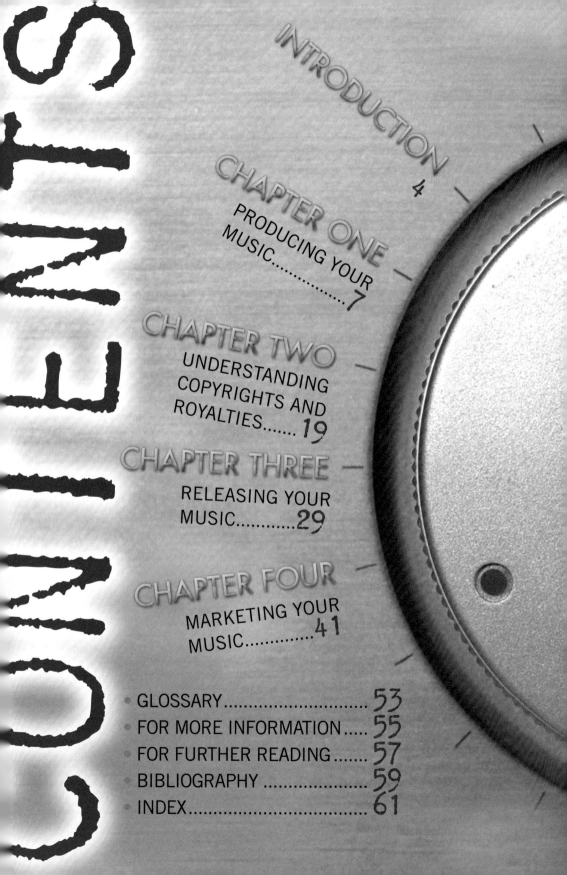

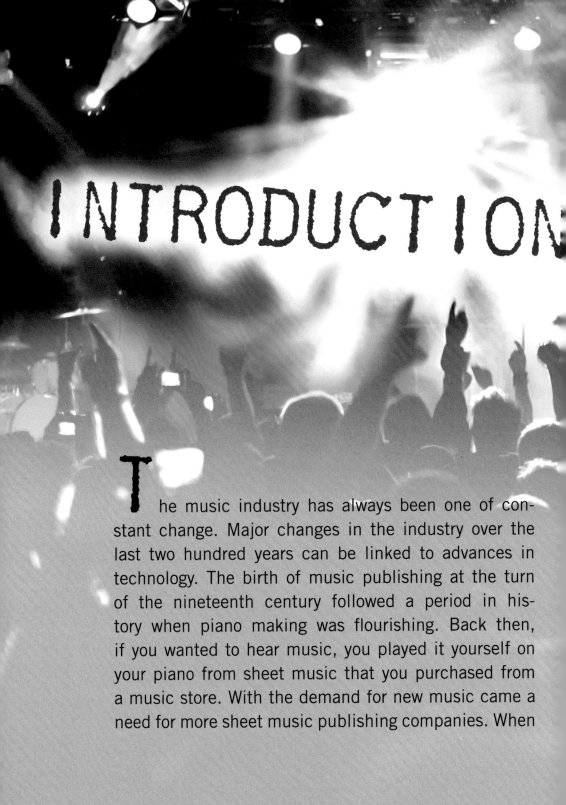

INTRODUCTION

The music industry has always been one of constant change. Major changes in the industry over the last two hundred years can be linked to advances in technology. The birth of music publishing at the turn of the nineteenth century followed a period in history when piano making was flourishing. Back then, if you wanted to hear music, you played it yourself on your piano from sheet music that you purchased from a music store. With the demand for new music came a need for more sheet music publishing companies. When

BANDS LIKE THE BOMBAY BICYCLE CLUB GOT THEIR START BY GAINING A FOLLOWING ONLINE AND USING THAT TO DRAW THE ATTENTION OF MAJOR RECORD LABELS.

Thomas Edison invented the phonograph in 1877, he was the first to record and reproduce sound. This opened the way for the beginning of the record industry.

By 1920, more than 150 companies were making records. And by the mid-1900s, record companies replaced sheet music publishing companies as the industry's major force. As technology advanced, records gave way to eight-track tapes, then to audiocassette tapes, and finally to CDs. Today, we have added digital music and the Internet to the mix. The CD business is shrinking as more and more people get their music through digital downloads on the Internet. With this technology has come more change.

It has never been so easy for young people to get their music heard. They are making this happen with nothing more than a few friends, a laptop, a few instruments, and a thriving MySpace page. They are building up an audience on the Internet and then gaining the attention of record companies. Groups like the Bombay Bicycle Club met at school in North London and were gathering interest from some of the country's top record labels before they even finished high school. Because the Internet links artists directly with their listeners and connects them with the services that they need to record, distribute, and promote their music, today's young artists, like the Bombay Bicycle Club, have more options than simply following the traditional paths of the music business. If you are a band that is just starting out, you have many exciting choices to make. This book will discuss some of the traditional ways and the newer ways that you can record, release, and market your music.

PRODUCING YOUR MUSIC

R ecording your music is important. A recording provides an archive for your band's evolution. It can also be used to generate income and promote you and your music. Years ago, musicians had no choice but to rent a professional recording studio in order to record their music. Today's musicians, though, have options when it comes to recording their music. A band can go the old-school route and record in a professional recording studio, or they can record in a home studio. However a band decides to record, there are four definite steps in the recording process.

CHAPTER
ONE
GARAGE
BAND
PASS

The Recording Process

The four steps in the recording process are preproduction, recording, mixing, and mastering. Before you actually record, it is important for you to plan. This is called preproduction. You must plan what you want to record, how you want to record it, who you want to do the recording, and what it is that you are hoping to achieve by recording it. Following preproduction, you are ready to record.

THE MIXER BALANCES, POSITIONS, EFFECTS, AND EQUALIZES DIFFERENT AUDIO CHANNELS INTO A GOOD-SOUNDING SONIC IMAGE, CALLED A MIX.

Recording is fun, but it is also a lot of work. It may take hours just to set up your equipment and tune your instruments, and you may have to do multiple takes for each song. When recording, multiple individual tracks are laid down. These tracks need to be edited and mixed together. During mixing, volumes can be adjusted, parts of a song can be deleted, and additions to the music can be made (such as the insertion of extra choruses).

The final step of the recording process is mastering. Mastering is when you make sure that everything in your song fits together.

HOW TO FIND A LOCAL RECORDING STUDIO

Musicians don't need to travel to a recording studio that is far away. You can probably find a decent place to record that is reasonably priced in your own home town. If money is an issue, it is probably wise to find someone near you who has built a studio in his or her home. Owners of home studios usually understand the financial constraints of a local band and their rates are usually much less expensive than larger studios. There are lots of home recording studios out there. The best way to locate one is to ask around. Other local bands may know of some that offer good quality and cheap prices.

Once you've found some local home studios, compare their prices. Ask about what kind of equipment and software they each use. They may also be able to provide you with a sample of their work. If you have never recorded before, you may also want to try to find a studio that charges per song instead of by the hour, since it may take longer to record your first time. Find out what kind of equipment the studios provide. Some home studios may be stocked with items such as drumsticks, tuners, cables, amplifiers, or even drum sets. Others may not.

9

Some of the fine-tuning that occurs during mastering may include the editing of minor flaws, volume adjustment, equalization of audio across the tracks, and elimination of hums, clicks, or hisses. It is during this step that your recording is polished and prepared for final release, whether that is digital downloading or CD duplication. Once you are done with the mastering process, your recording is complete.

In the Studio

Entering a big recording studio for the first time can be overwhelming. Studios have two main parts: the studio room, where the recording is made, and the engineering booth, where the sounds are recorded onto hard disc. When you rent a professional studio, you have access to all that the studio has to offer. You can use the professional recording equipment, such as the microphones, mixing board, hard disk setups, etc. The studio room has many different microphones on stands.

Mic cables snake across the floor in every direction. Studio rooms can be large enough to hold an entire orchestra or small enough for a solo guitarist. The price of a studio usually increases with size. The studio room is usually separated from the engineering booth by a large glass window. Inside the engineering booth, there is a large mixing board. All the microphones from the studio room are connected to the board.

RENTING A PROFESSIONAL RECORDING STUDIO GIVES AN ARTIST THE OPTION OF USING THE STUDIO'S OWN STAFF. SOME STUDIOS MAY EVEN PROVIDE PRODUCERS.

When you rent a professional recording studio, you also have the option of using the studio's own engineers. An engineer mans the mixing board, listening to the recording and adjusting the levels for each track, and determines what EQ (equalization) and effects are needed. An engineer also communicates with the musicians, providing them with feedback. Other engineers will do the mixing and mastering of the music.

11

Professional recording studios offer other professional staff and equipment as well. There are assistants who set up the instruments and position the mics. Most studios don't provide a producer, so you'll have to provide your own. The producer is basically the coach for a recording session. A producer helps decide what songs to record, how they should be performed, and who will play on each track. He or she also supervises the recording session and works closely with the engineers during the mixing and mastering processes.

Most studios also provide a variety of instruments that musicians can use. Many have a grand piano, drums, amps, and other instruments. Sometimes the use of these instruments is included in the studio rental fee. Other times, their use will cost extra.

The quality microphones, the experienced engineers, and the well-designed studio space all contribute to a professional-sounding recording. However, the use of a professional studio can be quite costly. It could cost from $50 to $150 per hour. The recording alone may end up costing up to $10,000. Postproduction (mixing and mastering) would probably add another few thousand to the cost. Since most studios charge by the hour, it is important to be prepared for your session beforehand. Have your songs prepared so that you don't have to work out the arrangements during valuable studio time. Make sure that you get a good night's sleep the night before your recording session so that you are rested and ready to work hard. Guitarists should bring new strings to the session, and drummers should bring new

TO GET YOUR MUSIC OUT THERE TODAY, YOU NEED ONLY GATHER SOME
BANDMATES, MAKE A DEMO ON A HOME COMPUTER, SET UP AN INTERNET
PAGE, AND ARRANGE SOME GIGS.

heads and sticks, just in case something breaks. You should
also make sure that the producers and engineers know what
sound you are looking for. You can even give them some examples ahead of time of the kind of styles you would like to see
reflected in your work. Finally, it is important to know when to
quit. Pushing a session too long will only make you tired and
cause your performance to suffer.

Your Home Studio

Musicians have been making home recordings for a long time. However, years ago, if artists wanted to make home recordings, they had to invest in lots of expensive recording equipment. Today, however, because of advances in computer processing, you can make a relatively high-quality recording at an affordable price. How much money you spend depends on what equipment you already have and what you have to purchase.

To record at home, you will need an adequate home computer. Your computer needs to be relatively fast so that it can handle all the digital audio processing. You should also have a lot of memory and a high-capacity hard drive.

To record your music, use a software program that functions as a digital audio workstation (DAW). A DAW uses computing power to take the place of traditional hardware. It allows you to record, edit, and play back. Essentially, the main part of your home studio exists in a virtual environment. Most computer-based DAWs have extensive MIDI recording, editing, and playback capabilities. Some even have minor video-related features. There are many affordable programs that you can run on your Mac or PC. However, Pro Tools is the most widely used recording and mixing software. Other options include Logic, GarageBand, and Cakewalk.

WITH THE WIDE SELECTION OF QUALITY MUSIC PRODUCTION SOFTWARE
AVAILABLE, IT IS EASY TO RECORD MULTIPLE TRACKS OF AUDIO ON
A COMPUTER.

Though you may be able to do without them, the best way to evaluate your recording would be a pair of quality, powered studio monitor speakers (the kind used in big studios). Monitoring speakers allow you to hear well and mix your project to be the very best. If you cannot afford these right away, very good headphones can serve as a reasonable substitute for the short term. Headphones are important when recording. They allow you to monitor what is being recorded through the system without hearing the other noises in the room. Each musician who is being recorded will need a pair.

If you are already performing live, you most likely have a few microphones. You could probably use these for recording, although higher-end mics that are designed specifically for recording would give you a more professional sound.

You will also need an audio interface unit. This piece of equipment handles the input and output of audio from your computer. Unless you are only recording one instrument at a time, you will need an audio interface unit with multiple inputs for guitars, keyboards, and microphones. If you are recording only one track at a time, you may be able to just use a single USB microphone instead of an audio interface box. This microphone connects to your computer via a USB connection. When it is all said and done, most people end up spending between $500 and $2,000 for a good-quality home recording setup.

PROFESSIONAL STUDIO MICROPHONES CAN COST THOUSANDS OF DOLLARS. HOWEVER, IT IS POSSIBLE TO FIND MICROPHONES OF DECENT QUALITY FOR A HOME STUDIO THAT COST SIGNIFICANTLY LESS.

Setting Up Your Home Recording Studio

The first step in setting up a home recording studio is to choose a room. The room you record and mix your music in can have as much effect on your finished product as your equipment. Try to find a room that is secluded from street noise and foot traffic. If possible, try to pick a room that is not square, is well-insulated, and has higher-than-normal ceilings. If need be, soundproof your studio by covering the inside walls and doors with plywood, studio foam, or sound blankets (or something similar to these). These will absorb sound waves, keeping them from bouncing back and forth between the walls.

Set up your computer on a table in the corner of the room, as far away as possible from where the musicians will be performing. Because it is physically difficult to play and engineer at the same time, it may be wise to recruit a friend to work the controls while you are playing. The way you set up your microphones really depends on personal taste. Place the microphones at various distances and positions until you hear from the studio monitors the sound you want. If you encounter poor room acoustics, try placing the microphone very close to the loudest part of the instrument.

UNDERSTANDING COPYRIGHTS AND ROYALTIES

If you have created a song, you should know the basics of copyright law. A copyright is the right given to the creator of a work to determine how that work will be used. When a work is copyrighted, the owner is given the right to decide who can publish it, copy it, and distribute it. A copyright protects you legally from any unauthorized use of your original works.

CHAPTER TWO

GARAGE BAND PASS

The Rights of a Copyright Owner

In order to understand the rights of a copyright owner, it is important to understand the difference between songs and sound recordings. A song (or musical work) refers to a melody, chords, and any accompanying lyrics. A sound recording is the recorded performance of someone else's song. A particular song may be recorded by many different artists. The U.S. Copyright Act of 1976 provides a copyright owner with six different types of rights, depending on the type of work involved. These are the right to make copies, distribute copies, prepare derivative works, perform publicly, perform publicly by digital audio transmission, and display the work publicly.

WEIRD AL YANKOVIC, KNOWN FOR HIS HUMOROUS SONGS, IS SHOWN HERE PERFORMING AT THE COMERICA CITYFEST ON JULY 5, 2007, IN DETROIT, MICHIGAN.

Both songwriters and makers of sound recordings have the right to make copies of their work. Not only can they make copies of the work, they can also distribute or sell these copies. No one else can copy or distribute these works without the copyright owner's permission. A copyright owner also controls the right to prepare derivative works. This right also applies to both songs and sound recordings.

A derivative work is a new creation based on an existing work. For example, in 1984, the performer Weird Al Yankovic released a song containing new lyrics for Michael Jackson's hit song "Beat It." But before Yankovic could release his song, which he called "Eat It," he had to obtain permission from Jackson. The right to perform publicly gives songwriters the right to perform their songs in public.

A public performance could be a live performance of a song by a cover band or the playing of a song recording on the radio. Sound recordings are not protected against being played publicly. They are, however, protected under the right to perform publicly by digital audio transmission. This performance right, which was created in 1995, applies to the playing of recordings on the Internet, on cable radio stations, and on satellite. The right to display publicly refers only to songs. It provides protection for the reproduction of music or lyrics on the Internet or in print.

TODAY'S GARAGE BANDS HAVE THE ABILITY TO BE DISCOVERED BY
THEIR OWN MEANS THROUGH ONLINE RELEASES AND DIRECT MARKETING
TO THEIR FANS. MUSIC SOFTWARE SUCH AS ITUNES MAKES IT EASY TO
INEXPENSIVELY DOWNLOAD MUSIC.

Making Money with Music

It is one thing to record, perform, or print your own music. But if you wish to use someone else's songs, you must pay the songwriter for the use of those songs. Likewise, if you have written a song that others would like to perform or record, they must pay you for the right to do so. These payments, made to a holder of a copyright, are called royalties. In addition to establishing legal ownership of a work, a copyright also determines royalties. A copyright holder can receive royalties by issuing a license that allows the copyrighted work to be used by someone else. There are five different types of licenses: mechanical licenses, performance licenses, synchronization licenses, print licenses, and foreign licenses. The type of license required depends on how the work will be used. If your band does not write its own music, the licenses that are more likely to affect you are mechanical licenses and performance licenses.

Mechanical licenses are issued for the use of songs. If a person wishes to reproduce (or record) a song on CD, digital download, or some other kind of media, he or she must pay mechanical royalties to the copyright holder. If you are planning on recording a song that someone else has written, you must obtain a mechanical license and pay royalties to that songwriter for each copy of the recording that you sell. The nation's leading provider of licensing services in the music industry is the Harry Fox Agency (HFA). If you are recording your band playing someone else's songs, contact the HFA and request a mechanical license. The agency will walk you through the process. Likewise, if you are a songwriter, you will collect royalties if someone else records your song.

The Role of a Publisher

By creating a copyright, you not only have rights as the owner of the work but also rights as the music publisher. A music publisher is a company that owns song copyrights. A music publisher controls how a song will be used and collects money (royalties) from people who perform or sell the song. A songwriter can either remain his or her own publishing company or sell the song to a music publisher. Usually, a music publisher will receive about 60 to 75 percent of a song's income.

Do you need a publisher? If your goal as a songwriter is to have other artists perform your songs, you may want to consider signing with a publishing company. In this case, a publisher will work to promote your songs to other artists. This is important because publishers often have a lot of contacts in the music industry. If you sign with a publishing company, you will work with whichever performing rights organization it is affiliated with. However, if you are a songwriter who only writes songs for you and your band to perform, you probably do not need a publisher. In this case, you will need to partner with one of the performing rights organizations. The organization you choose will collect royalties for you, and you can keep all the money for yourself.

HAPPY BIRTHDAY TO YOU

Have you ever wondered why restaurants, like Applebee's, make up their own songs to sing for patrons' birthdays instead of just singing the tried-and-true "Happy Birthday to You"? It is because of copyright laws. "Happy Birthday to You" was copyrighted in 1934 by the Hill family. Two sisters, Mildred J. Hill and Patty Smith Hill, had developed the tune to the song in 1893. It originally had the lyrics "Good morning to you," a simple greeting song for kindergarteners to sing to their teachers. The copyright currently belongs to Warner Music Group, which charges up to $30,000 for the use of the song in movies, as ringtones, or in any other public setting. Don't worry, though—it is perfectly legal to sing "Happy Birthday" to your family and friends in the privacy of your own home.

A performance license gives a person the right to perform a song in public. The writer of the song would then be paid performance royalties for the use of that song. Because the makers of sound recordings are not covered under the right to perform publicly, they do not have the right to collect royalties if their recordings are used.

Any time you play music that you have not written (whether live or recorded) in a public place, performance royalties must be paid to the songwriters of the songs. The good news is that the venue where you are playing (such as a club, lounge, or concert hall) will pay the performance royalties for you. Once again, if you are the songwriter, performers would be paying you for the right to perform your song in public. Every time a song is played on the radio, on television, in a live concert, or in a business establishment, the people playing the song must pay for it. In the United States, there are three organizations that monitor the performances of songs on the radio, in nightclubs, on television, and on Web sites. They collect royalties and distribute them to the appropriate people. These performance rights organizations are the American Society of Composers, Authors, and Publishers (ASCAP), Broadcast Music, Inc. (BMI), and the Society of European Stage Authors and Composers (SESAC).

How to Copyright Your Music

You don't actually have to file anything with the government to obtain a copyright. This is because in the United States, a song is copyrighted as soon as you write it and a recording is copyrighted as soon as you record it. Why should you bother filing a copyright then? It is still wise to register a copyright for your work because it provides the best proof of ownership. You can register a copyright online by visiting the Web site for the U.S. Copyright Office (http://www.copyright.gov). By registering your copyright, you are providing yourself with extra protection in case someone infringes on your work.

Copyright Infringement

Copyrights are not just valuable for their ability to establish ownership. They are also necessary for collecting royalties when other artists use your song or recording. If a work is used without permission, it is called copyright infringement. When you write a song, it belongs to you. As the owner, you are entitled to all of the royalties due for the use of the song. If someone else uses the melody of your song without your permission, that is stealing, and you are due any royalties that the person would collect for that song.

THE WEB SITE FOR THE U.S. COPYRIGHT OFFICE (HTTP://WWW.COPYRIGHT.GOV) PROVIDES LINKS FOR INFORMATION ABOUT COPYRIGHT LAW, ONLINE COPYRIGHT RECORDS, AND FORMS FOR REGISTERING A COPYRIGHT ONLINE.

One of the most well-known copyright infringement cases involved former Beatles guitarist George Harrison. It was alleged that the melody from his 1969 song "My Sweet Lord" was taken from a song made popular by the Chiffons in 1963, called "He's So Fine." The trial lasted for five years, and Harrison was eventually found guilty of copyright infringement. He was ordered to pay $587,000 to the original song's copyright owner.

Copyright infringement is a murky area of law, and a violation is often hard to pinpoint. In the case involving Harrison, the court actually acknowledged that he may have copied the song unintentionally.

RELEASING YOUR MUSIC

CHAPTER THREE

GARAGE BAND PASS

Years ago, the only way to really get your music out there or to sell it was by signing a deal with a major record label. Therefore, obtaining a contract with one of these companies was the ultimate goal for many musicians, artists, and bands. There used to be a large number of major labels out there. But due to the changing music industry, there are only four major record companies left. These companies, called the Big Four, include EMI Group, Sony BMG Entertainment, Universal Music Group (UMG), and Warner Music Group (WMG). With the advances in digital technology and the rise of the Internet, many more options exist for today's artists. One alternative is to sign with a

TWO OF THE BIG FOUR MAJOR RECORD COMPANIES ARE EMI AND SONY BMG. SONY BMG IS THE RESULT OF THE 2004 MERGER BETWEEN SONY MUSIC ENTERTAINMENT AND BERTELSMANN MUSIC GROUP.

smaller, independent label. Other artists simply choose to release their own music, either physically or digitally. Though today's artists have more choices, some still feel it is in their best interest to sign with a major label.

The Pros and Cons of Signing with a Major Label

The main thing that a major label has to offer is money. A major label is like a one-stop shop. It handles the entire music-making process. Once you've signed with a major label, the company will loan you money for your recording, and it will pay for the production and distribution of your CDs. Finally, it takes care of the promotion. The label will take out ads in newspapers and music magazines, and it will run commercials on radio stations. The company may also pay to have a Web site created for you or have promotional merchandise produced for you.

Some record labels may offer you an advance when you sign a contract. Though you must pay this money back once you have generated some royalties, it helps you get started. In addition to money, major labels are also useful for the connections they offer. The connections that they have formed over the decades can help you reach your music career goals. They can also pull some major strings when it comes to the media, such as getting you an interview with a big music magazine.

Having one of the major record labels working on your music may be your ticket to the big time. However, there are some downsides to signing with a major label as well. Once a record deal is made, the label would most likely own the music's copyright. This means that the label would receive the royalties and would pay you, the artist, a

DO WELL-ESTABLISHED PERFORMERS NEED BIG MUSIC CONGLOMERATES IN
THE DIGITAL AGE? BANDS LIKE RADIOHEAD DO NOT SEEM TO THINK SO.
THEY HAVE TAKEN TO SELLING THEIR OWN ALBUMS ON THE INTERNET.

certain percentage. Since the label is investing so much in you, it will also want a say in what you do—from the songs you include on your album to the musicians you use when recording to the places you tour. If you sign with a major label, you may be giving up a lot of creative control.

The Pros and Cons of Signing with an Independent Label

Today, signing with a major record label is not your only choice. One other option is signing with an independent label. An independent (or indie) label is any record label that is not affiliated in any way with any of the four major record labels. Indie labels do most of the same things that a major record label would do, but on a smaller scale. An independent label would still take care of the business and distribution, but it would allow the artist to retain more creative control and would cost less than a major label. Instead of taking care of promotion themselves, indie labels would probably contract that responsibility out. As with a major label, you will have expenses taken out of your royalties that will go to the label. You will also have to pay back any advance you may receive before you see a royalty check. However, it is usually easier to negotiate the terms of a contract with an indie label.

The real difference between a major record label and an independent one is seen in the relationship between the label and the artist. With an independent label, you are dealing with a handful of people instead of a large company. You will be able to work with and form closer relationships with the people at the label. If you have a problem, you are more likely to be able to just pick up the phone and speak to someone in charge than you would if you were working with a major label. Since an indie label will be working with fewer artists than a major label, you may also get more promotional attention. An indie label has the freedom to work with whomever it chooses. It doesn't have the pressure to go against

BEFORE YOU SIGN

Before you sign a contract, go over it with a manager and an attorney—everything a label offers is negotiable. Since a major label works with so many artists, you may find yourself competing for attention. Major labels tend to sign a lot of musicians and then throw the music out there to see what sticks. If your music isn't bringing in a lot of money, the label may not continue to waste its time and money promoting it. Though many dedicated music lovers work with major labels, some who work for them do not love music. They are in it strictly for the money. This is a major difference when compared to independent labels.

what it likes in favor of what may be successful in the mainstream market. Therefore, if an indie label has signed with you, it most likely means that it did so because it really likes your music. Because it believes in what you're doing, it may work a little harder to promote it.

Though the small size of an indie label provides a more intimate working relationship, its size also has its disadvantages. While an abundance of money is an advantage for a major label, lack of money is definitely a disadvantage for an indie label. An indie label does not have the money to boost a new release as well as a major label can. If you work with an indie label, do not expect radio commercials and magazine ads. You may even be asked to help out with the promotional work. Because an indie label has less money, you may not receive an advance. This means that you would simply be living off of royalty payments. You may also need to cover some of the recording costs. Indie labels are more accepting of home-based recordings, though, so the artists are not stuck with huge studio bills and producers fees. Overall, with an indie label, you are trading less money up front for a more personal experience in the long run.

Distributing Your Own Music

Digital technology enables artists to inexpensively record their music in their own homes. Therefore, they no longer need the financial backing of a label. This opens up a third option for artists—distributing their music themselves. After recording and burning their own CDs, artists have several options for distributing them. First, an artist can sell CDs on his or her own Web site or at a live performance.

If artists would like to distribute their CDs on a greater scale, they can look into selling them in a traditional record store. In order to do this, an artist would have to locate and sign a deal with a record distributor. There are several types of record distributors in the United States. One type of distributor, called a rack jobber, leases space in other retail stores and usually carries only the best-selling products. Rack jobbers concentrate on CDs from the major labels. One-stop distributors carry a variety of products from both major and independent labels. They sell them to independent record shops, chain stores, and other outlets. Independent distributors distribute CDs from indie

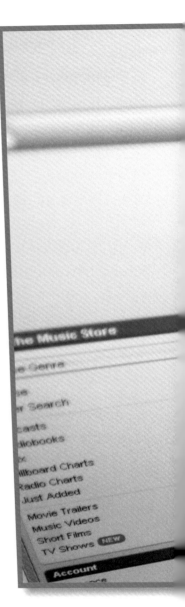

APPLE'S ITUNES (HTTP://WWW.ITUNES.COM) IS A GREAT PLACE FOR
GARAGE BANDS TO DISTRIBUTE THEIR MUSIC. ITUNES HAS MILLIONS
OF SONGS FOR DOWNLOAD, MANY FOR UNDER A DOLLAR.

labels and individual artists to retail outlets. You should probably start with an independent distributor if you are attempting to release your own CD.

Distributors function as middlemen. Retail stores pay them, and they pay the record label. When a distributor sells a CD for you, that distributor will give you approximately 50 percent of the suggested list price. Some examples of the larger distributors in the United States are Alternative Distribution Alliance, E1 Entertainment Distribution, Fontana Distribution, and Redeye Distribution. More information about these can be found in the "For More Information" section at the end of this book.

An artist can also sell music online as physical CDs or as digital downloads. Although you could try on your own to get your music on download sites, like iTunes, there are services that will do that for you. Two such services are TuneCore and CD Baby. For their service, both TuneCore and CD Baby charge fees upfront. However, they do all the work to get your music listed with digital stores such as iTunes, Amazon MP3, emusic, Zune, and Thumbplay.

When you make a sale with one of these online stores, each store will keep a certain percentage of your sale money. This percentage varies per store. On top of that, CD Baby will take an additional 9 percent of the net income paid to it by these stores. Tunecore, on the other hand, allows you to keep all the revenues that you earn at each store. However, while Tunecore charges an annual subscription fee and annual fees pertaining to the sale of singles ($9.99 per single), ringtones ($9.99 per ringtone), and albums ($49.99 per album the first year, and $19.98 each additional year), CD Baby charges no such annual fees.

Though digital downloads are becoming increasingly important and are quickly supplanting the CD business, CDs are not dead yet. It is still important to make the purchase of physical CDs an option for fans. Therefore, it is notable that Tunecore and CD Baby both offer CD printing and distribution. Tunecore offers this service on Amazon. You can select the sale price for your album (between $8.98 and $19.98), but you will receive only 40 percent of the price selected. For example, if you choose to sell your album for $10.98, you will receive $4.39. CD Baby also allows you to set your own sale prices. When your albums sell, it keeps $4 for every CD sold, and you keep the rest. If you sold your album for $10.98 on CD Baby, you would keep $6.98 of that.

When you choose to release your own album, you get to decide how your music is used, when it is used, and how much people will have to pay for it. You don't have to worry about giving up your vision, creativity, or style. You also don't have to give up your cash to a record label. However, when you decide not to go with a record label, you are giving up a possible advance. Labels do initially pick up the costs of releasing an album. If you release your own album, you will have to cover these initial costs out of pocket. Labels also have established contacts that help them promote releases. It will take time and energy to build your own network of connections. Releasing your own album is a full-time job. You must do all of the jobs of a record label—production, distribution, and marketing. Though this may seem like a daunting task, it is nice to know that you have a choice.

MARKETING YOUR MUSIC

CHAPTER
FOUR

You have your band, possibly played some gigs, and maybe even recorded your music. What you need to do now is get your name out there. You want your band and your music to be recognized. Just as you need to give people a way to purchase your music, you need to let them know that you exist in the first place. If you choose to work with a record label, it will take care of the marketing and promotion of your album. If you prefer to remain independent, you also have the option of hiring an independent record promoter. However, there are lots of ways that you can promote your music yourself. Some of these include print advertising, radio advertising, online promotion, and merchandise sales.

Promoting with Flyers

Even if your goal is to play in local clubs and coffeehouses, you still need promotion. For local advertisement, one of the most tried-and-trusted tools is a flyer. Fortunately, this method of promotion is also inexpensive. You can print up several hundred flyers for less than $30. You can hand-write or draw your flyer, or you can use your computer. It helps if your flyer has catchy graphics or photos.

To make it look somewhat professional, you may want to contract an artist or designer friend to do the work. There are also online sites, such as PrintPlace.com, where you can upload your artwork to create a flyer. This might cost you between $100 and $200. When designing your flyer, be sure to include your band's Web address if you have a Web site, and include any information pertaining to an upcoming gig. Also make sure that the most important information stands out and can be seen from a distance.

Once you've created your flyers, you and your band should be able to distribute them without incurring any further costs. Before you head out to place your flyers, take a minute to think about where music fans are likely to gather in your area. You'll probably get the most attention by placing your flyers at local music stores, coffeehouses, and record stores. If there is a college nearby, that may be a good place to put some flyers as well. Look for places on campus where there is a lot of student traffic.

GRAPHIC DESIGN PROGRAMS, SUCH AS ADOBE ILLUSTRATOR AND ADOBE PHOTOSHOP, CAN BE USED TO INEXPENSIVELY DESIGN PROMOTIONAL FLYERS.

Print Advertising

You could potentially spend a lot of money on print advertising. National newspapers and magazines could cost thousands or tens of thousands of dollars. Therefore, unless you have an extremely large budget, you will not be able to consider national print advertising. However, even on a smaller budget, you should be able to afford some types of print advertising, such as weekly alternative papers, college newspapers, and local newspapers.

Advertising in weekly alternative papers is pretty cost-effective. These papers usually highlight local people and culture, and they are targeted toward younger audiences. Colleges usually have their own newspapers and would be a good choice because college students are a prime music-buying group. You may be able to purchase a small ad in your local weekly newspaper or college newspaper for a few hundred dollars. It may cost a little more for a daily local paper.

Radio Advertising and Radio Play

If you're thinking about trying to advertise your music on the radio but you don't have a large budget, think local. When you are deciding which radio stations to approach, it makes sense to choose the ones that play your type of music. For example, if you're a rap artist, you wouldn't want to advertise your music on a country station. As with print advertising, college radio stations are probably the most effective and inexpensive choice for radio advertising. College stations are at the heart of breaking new music, and they are usually eager to support local artists. They might be willing to play your demo CD on air or even have you come to the station for an interview or live performance.

TRADITIONAL RADIO ADVERTISING IS A GOOD OPTION FOR INDEPENDENT ARTISTS. COLLEGE RADIO STATIONS ARE USUALLY QUITE WILLING TO PROMOTE NEW MUSIC FROM LOCAL UP-AND-COMING ARTISTS.

Radio play such as this is probably the most traditional form of music promotion. Independent artists can gain great exposure for their music on college radio stations or on independent stations (nonprofit stations that are not directly affiliated with any radio network, school, company, or government). However, without a major label, most artists cannot afford the cost required to get the big corporate stations that are found in most major cities to play their music.

Web sites like Radio-Locator can help independent artists locate some stations that may be a good fit for them. With Radio-Locator, you can search for stations by area and then narrow your search by music genre. The site provides the contact information for each of

PROMOTING YOURSELF

Justin Bieber's launch into superstardom started when he posted some homemade music videos on YouTube in 2007. Bieber was discovered when a marketing executive named Scooter Braun stumbled upon his online videos in 2008 and tracked him down. In 2008, Bieber officially signed a record deal with Island Records.

Most artists today also use social networks like MySpace, Twitter, or Facebook to get information out about themselves. Such online tools allow artists to communicate directly with the people who care about their music. This type of one-to-one relationship is not possible with traditional advertising. Posting a message on Twitter or MySpace is easy and does not have to be time-consuming. However, to keep fans happy and interested, an artist must keep the lines of communication open. If you go more than a week without blogging or tweeting, fans will lose interest and fall away. MySpace is probably the most suited to musicians.

You can use the site's tools to create your own home page on the site for free. On your page, you can include details about your band, photos, and a calendar of upcoming shows. There is also a place for your friends and fans to make comments and a place for you to write your own blogs. It is also possible to sell your music, in the form of downloadable MP3 files, on MySpace. Facebook is becoming more user-friendly for musicians as well. With Facebook, you can create a fan page that allows you to promote your music and performances to your friends and fans.

the stations so that you can get in touch with them. Once you have decided which radio stations to target, you must get your music and information to the right people at these stations. One of the best ways to do this is by creating a press kit.

Most online advertising is a lot less expensive than traditional television, radio, and print advertising. This makes it affordable for most independent artists. The three most common ways in which online advertising is purchased are CPM (cost per mille), CPC (cost per click), and CPA (cost per action). With CPM, advertisers pay each time a user clicks on their listing and is redirected to their Web site. With CPC, advertisers pay to be listed under a series of target words that direct users to their Web site. They pay only when someone clicks on the listing that leads directly to their site. With CPA, advertisers pay only for the amount of users that complete a transaction, such as making a purchase.

Years ago, musicians had little choice in the way they got their music to the public. Today, because of technological advances, artists have multiple options every step along the way. From the recording to the releasing to the marketing of their music, they can choose which parts of the process they would like to do themselves and what they would rather pay someone else to do. Having all of these options may mean that, to be successful in today's music business, musicians like you have to be as creative in business as you are with your music.

Creating a Press Kit

A press kit is a tool used by musicians to provide visual, physical, and audio information about their band and their music. It is a good idea to create your press kit in both digital and paper form. Press kits are an important part of a lot of things you will need to do as a band, from the self-promotion of your music to getting a gig to approaching a record label. Some press kits are very simple, while others contain a lot of bells and whistles. Your press kit should definitely include the following: your band's bio, your demo CD, copies of any press the band has received, and your contact information.

Your bio should be a one-page background of you or your band. This should be typed and free of spelling errors. Keep your bio short and to the point, but make sure that you let the recipient know about your current CD and why it should be listened to. Your demo CD should be just that—a demonstration of your music.

Pick your best two or three songs to include. Anything longer than that will not get listened to. Since you are including only a few songs, picking the right songs is important. It is a good idea to pick songs that have strong beginnings because your songs will be given only a few seconds to make an impression before someone presses the "Next" button. Include with your CD a track list that gives the song titles, songwriter info, and the artist name. If your band has received any press, include the press clippings in your press kit, too.

Now is the time to highlight your band's achievements. Make a copy of each press clipping on a separate piece of paper and bind the pages together. Finally, make sure you include your contact information in your press kit. Nothing would be worse than having someone like your work with no way to contact you about it. Include your e-mail address, phone number, and postal address. If you have any online resources, such as a MySpace page or video on YouTube, include the URLs so that the recipient of your press kit can check those out, too.

Once you have finished your press kit, it is important to send it to the right people. If you are sending it to a radio station or record label, make sure that it deals with your type of music. You may also need to address your demo to a specific person in order for it to be heard. Some labels, especially the larger ones, will not even accept unsolicited demos. Check out the Web sites for the labels you are targeting and see what their demo policies are and how you should send your package.

After you have sent your press kit to a radio station, local reviewer, potential gig, or record label, you should follow up personally. Wait a week or two and then call or e-mail them to find out if they have received your material. If they have received it and listened to it, find out what they think about it. If there is a lack of interest from the recipient, be polite and ask if they have any advice for you. They may even know of someone else who may be interested. Keep a list of everyone you send your press kit to and everyone you talk to about your demo. If someone was not interested in your demo, you do not necessarily need to take them off your list. You may be able to revisit this contact when something new comes up, such as a new song. You never know who will be able to help you out down the line. And next time, they might just say yes.

Promoting Your Music Online

Aside from the more traditional promotional activities already discussed, today's artists can utilize the Internet to advertise their music. Online promotional tools such as e-mail, blogs, Web sites, social networks, and online advertising are effective and cost less (or sometimes nothing at all) than most traditional modes of advertisement. By adding your fans to an e-mail mailing list, you can keep them updated on new albums you'll be releasing or concerts you'll be playing. You may also want to add to your e-mail list the people to whom you've sent your press kit. You could even use e-mail to get your virtual press kits where they need to go. Send e-mails only to people you have come into contact with or that have shown interest in your music. You can get names and addresses for your e-mail list by having a sign-up sheet at your gigs or by creating an e-mail sign-up form on your Web site.

THERE ARE MANY SOCIAL NETWORKS OUT THERE THAT CAN HELP YOU PRO-
MOTE YOUR BAND AND YOUR MUSIC BUSINESS. SOME OF THE MOST POPULAR
ARE VIMEO (HTTP://WWW.VIMEO.COM), FACEBOOK (HTTP://WWW.FACEBOOK.
COM), TWITTER (HTTP://WWW.TWITTER.COM), LINKEDIN (HTTP://WWW.
LINKEDIN.COM), AND YOUTUBE (HTTP://WWW.YOUTUBE.COM).

Anyone can easily and inexpensively publish a blog or create a Web site. Creating your own Web site or blog offers a way to communicate with fans and keep them informed. Blogs are great for posting your latest announcements or news. Creating your own Web site gives you even more options. Not only can musicians give details about their latest news and happenings, they can also post information about themselves, photos, and videos.

Web sites make it possible for artists to further promote themselves by offering free downloads of their music. If artists would like to sell their music, they can also create pages on their site to sell CDs and other merchandise, such as T-shirts. A Web site's blog page would offer an artist the opportunity to periodically talk to fans. Artists can also create a press page where favorable articles and reviews that have been written about them can be posted. If you need help designing a site, there are a lot of designers out there. It could cost a few thousand dollars for a decent-sized Web site with a good design. There are also Internet tools that can help you set up a Web site. One example is Bandzoogle. This tool helps musicians with little or no Web design skills build and maintain a band Web site for a monthly fee of between $10 and $20.

GLOSSARY

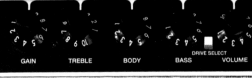

AUDIO   Relating to humanly audible sounds.

COPYRIGHT   The rights granted by law to the creator of an original work.

DERIVATIVE WORK   A new musical work based on one or more already existing works.

DIGITAL AUDIO WORKSTATION (DAW)   A software program that enables you to record music on your computer to a digital file.

DIGITAL RECORDING   A recording in which the audio is stored in the form of binary digits (ones and zeros).

DISTRIBUTOR   A company that distributes products to individual retail stores. It serves as a middleman between the record label or artist and the retail store.

DOWNLOAD   To obtain a song or track (in the form of a digital audio file) from a Web site.

EQUALIZATION   The process of boosting or cutting audio signals at a specific frequency or range of frequencies.

INPUT   The connection going into an audio device.

LICENSE   The official permission to use a copyrighted work.

MARKETING   The act of promoting and selling products.

MIDI RECORDING   MIDI stands for musical instrument digital interface. It is software designed to let different instruments communicate with each other electronically.

MIXING BOARD   A device that mixes or combines audio signals and controls the relative levels of the signals.

OUTPUT   A connector in an audio device from which the signal comes. It feeds into other devices.

PREPRODUCTION   The planning that takes place before a recording.

PRESS KIT   A package of promotional material.

PROMOTE   To spread information about a product.

ROYALTY   The payment made to a copyright holder for the use of the copyrighted work.

SOUNDPROOF   To prevent the passage of sound into or out of an area.

SOUND RECORDING   The recorded performance of a song.

TAKE   A sound recording made during a single recording period. Usually, several takes are done of each song, and the best parts of each take are used in the final product.

TRACK   An audio component that contains the performance of one musical instrument.

CD Baby
13909 NE Airport Way
Portland, OR 97230
(503) 595-3000
Web site: http://www.cdbaby.com
CD Baby specializes in the physical and digital distribution
of music from independent labels and independent
artists.

E1 Entertainment Distribution
22 Harbor Park Drive
Port Washington, NY 11050
Web site: http://www.e1distribution.com
E1 is an independent music and video distribution company.
It offers physical and digital distribution for independent
record labels and studios.

Fontana Distribution
111 Universal Hollywood Drive, Suite 500
Universal City, CA 91608
(877) 878-FONTANA [366-8262]
Web site: http://www.fontanadistribution.com
Fontana Distribution provides full-service, worldwide distribution for independent labels. It offers physical sales and
marketing with production, manufacturing, warehousing,

and facilities support. It also offers digital, video, and mobile setup, distribution, and marketing.

Redeye Distribution
449-A Trollingwood Road
Haw River, NC 27258
(877) RED-EYE1 [733-3931]
Web site: http://www.redeyeusa.com
Redeye Distribution provides a physical and digital distribution network both nationally and internationally for independent record labels.

TuneCore
45 Washington Street, Box #256
Brooklyn, NY 11201
Web site: http://www.tunecore.com
TuneCore is a digital music distribution service. It offers musicians the opportunity to place their music into digital retailers. It differs from traditional digital music distribution in that it takes no percentage of a customer's sales, does not ask for copyright rights, and does not require exclusivity.

Web Sites

Due to the changing nature of Internet links, Rosen Publishing has developed an online list of Web sites related to the subject of this book. This site is updated regularly. Please use this link to access the list:

http://www.rosenlinks.com/gaba/prod

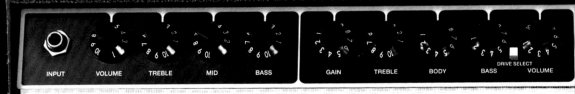

Azzarelli, Ally. *Justin Bieber: Teen Music Superstar* (Hot Celebrity Biographies). Berkeley Heights, NJ: Enslow Publishers, 2011.

Bidini, Dave. *For Those About to Rock: A Road Map to Being in a Band*. Plattsburgh, NY: Tundra Books, 2004.

Bliesener, Mark. *The Complete Idiot's Guide to Starting a Band*. New York, NY: Penguin Group, 2006.

Buttwinick, Marty. *Starting Your First Band* (The Musicians How-To Series). Glendale, CA: Sonta Publishing, 2008.

Chertkow, Randy. *The Indie Band Survival Guide: The Complete Manual for the Do-It-Yourself Musician*. New York, NY: St. Martin's Press, 2008.

Cook, John. *Our Noise: The Story of Merge Records, the Indie Label That Got Big and Stayed Small*. Chapel Hill, NC: Algonquin Books, 2009.

Du Noyer, Paul, ed. *The Billboard Illustrated Encyclopedia of Music*. New York, NY: Billboard Books, 2003.

Espejo, Roman, ed. *Copyright Infringement*. Farmington Hills, MI: Greenhaven Press, 2009.

Goodmark, Robyn. *Girls Rock: How to Get Your Group Together and Make Some Noise*. New York, NY: Billboard Books, 2008.

Hagerman, Andrew. *Digital Music Making for Teens*. Boston, MA: Thomas Course Technology PTR, 2004.

Hopper, Jessica. *The Girls' Guide to Rocking: How to Start a Band, Book Gigs, and Get Rolling to Rock Stardom*. New York, NY: Workman Publishing Company, 2009.

King, Mike. *Music Marketing: Press, Promotion, Distribution, and Retail*. Milwaukee, WI: Hal Leonard Corporation, 2009.

Krasilovsky, William. *This Business of Music*. 8th ed. New York, NY: Billboard Books, 2000.

Potts, Kimberly. *Kidz Bop: Be a Popstar! Start Your Own Band, Book Your Own Gigs, and Become a Rock and Roll Phenom!*. Cincinnati, OH: Adams Media, 2011.

Rod, Gervias. *Home Recording Studio: Build It Like the Pros*. Boston, MA: Thomas Course Technology PTR, 2006.

Schwartz, Daylle Deanna. *Start and Run Your Own Record Label*. 3rd ed. New York, NY: Billboard Books, 2009.

BIBLIOGRAPHY

Anderson, Marisa, ed. *Rock'n' Roll Camp for Girls: How to Start a Band, Write Songs, Record an Abum, and Rock Out*. San Francisco, CA: Chronicle Books, 2008.

Borg, Bobby. *The Musician's Handbook: A Practical Guide to Understanding the Music Business*. New York, NY: Billboard Books, 2008.

Garage Band Academy. "Garage Band Academy." 2011. Retrieved March 31, 2011.

Harris, Sarah. "Too Cool for School: The Teen Bands Who've Got the Music Industry on the Run." *Independent*, May 20, 2007. Retrieved March 31, 2011 (http://www. independent.co.uk/arts-entertainment/music/features/ too-cool-for-school-the-teen-bands-whove-got-the-music- industry-on-the-run-449053.html).

Johnson, Arne, and Karen Macklin. *Indie Girl*. San Francisco, CA: Zest Books, 2008.

Lowry, Heidi. "Famous Copyright Infringement in the Music Industry." Suite101.com, June 2, 2010. Retrieved March 31, 2011 (http://www.suite101.com/content/famous- copyright-infringement-cases-in-the-music-industry- a243968).

Maschino, Shawn. "Studio Building & Display." HomeRecording.com, 2011. Retrieved March 31, 2011 (http://homerecording.com/bbs/general-discussions/ studio-building-display).

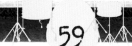

McDonald, Heather. "Bands/Musicians." About.com, 2011. Retrieved March 31, 2011 (http://musicians.about.com/od/beingamusician/u/BandsandMusicians.htm).

McDonald, Heather. "Understanding Contracts and Copyrights." About.com, 2011. Retrieved March 31, 2011 (http://musicians.about.com/od/resources/u/Understanding-Contracts-And-Copyrights.htm).

Miller, Michael. *The Complete Idiot's Guide to the Music Business.* New York, NY: Penguin Group, 2010.

Naggar, David. *The Music Business* (Explained in Plain English). San Francisco, CA: DaJé Publishing, 2004.

Passman, Donald. *All You Need to Know About the Music Business.* 6th ed. New York, NY: Free Press, 2006.

Stim, Rich. *Music Law: How to Run Your Band's Business.* 6th ed. Berkeley, CA: Nolo, 2009.

INDEX

About the Author

Heather Hasan loves music. She enjoys playing the piano, clarinet, tenor saxophone, and harmonica. Her husband, Omar, plays the drums in a worship band. They live in Durham, North Carolina, with their three children, Samuel, Matthew, and Sarah.

Photo Credits

Cover © www.istockphoto.com/Chris Schmidt; cover and interior background image (club), pp. 8, 17, 45 Shutterstock.com; p. 5 Ollie Millington/Redferns/Getty Images; p. 11 Digital Vision/Thinkstock; p. 13 Jupiterimages/Photos.com/Thinkstock; p. 15 Nicole Russo; p. 20 Paul Warner/WireImage/Getty Images; p. 22 © Photononstop/SuperStock; p. 30 (top) Shaun Curry/AFP/Getty Images; p. 30 (bottom) Bloomberg via Getty Images; pp. 32–33 Jim Steinfeldt/Michael Ochs Archives/Getty Images; pp. 36–37 Bloomberg via Getty Images; p. 43 © Brigette Sullivan/PhotoEdit; p. 51 © www.istockphoto.com/Luca Cepparo; back cover and interior graphic elements © www.istockphoto.com/Adam Gryko (radio dial), © www.istockphoto.com/Tomasz Zajaczkowski (amp), © www.istockphoto.com/sammyc (drum set silhouette), Shutterstock.com (cable, frequency bar), © www.istockphoto.com/spxChrome (stage pass), © www.istockphoto.com/Bryan Faust (foot pedal).

Designer: Nicole Russo; Editor: Nicholas Croce;
Photo Researcher: Karen Huang